Selling Emotionally Transformative Services Companion Notebook

Thought-Provoking Questions to Integrate and Apply to Your Business

Todd Schaefer

How to Use This Book

Greetings Non-traditional Business Owner!

The purpose of this companion notebook is to integrate into your mind and business practices the ideas and principles you've already read in my book, Selling Emotionally Transformative Services (S.E.T.S.): Business and Self-Worth Advice Holistic Practitioners Need to Know (available on Amazon).

In this companion notebook, you will find two primary things: 1) thought-provoking business questions derived from the SETS book, and 2) plenty of notebook space to write your reflections. Questions in this notebook are purposefully phrased and carefully worded. Some questions have correct answers defined in the SETS book while other questions are purely for encouraging self-reflection and personal growth. I'll let you discover which is which.

As a recommended daily practice, read only one thought-provoking question per day, contemplate it, refer back to and reread relevant content in the SETS book if desired, and take ample time to journal your reflections and answers in the companion notebook. I can guarantee that if you journal about only one question per day, it will provide maximal absorption and integration of the materials (as opposed to rushing through it). Since this companion notebook's questions are posed at random, it's recommended to read the SETS book first, and then begin the daily practice of the companion notebook.

I encourage you to use the additional space provided to take notes, record new personal and professional insights, set goals and action steps for your business, and stay accountable to acting on them. You can also use this notebook to record business development ideas, networking contacts and more.

Once you have completely finished answering the questions in the notebook, review it again to ensure you have implemented everything I have recommended in the SETS book and in this companion notebook for best results.

To Your Success,

Todd Schaefer

You can overcome anything if you know why you're doing it and you break it down into a series of steps. Take a current challenge and practice breaking it down into smaller steps.

_____

_____

_____

_____

_____

_____

_____

_____

_____

_____

_____

_____

_____

_____

_____

_____

_____

_____

_____

_____

_____

_____

_____

Notes:

Business Ideas

Goals

Action Steps

Successes

There is no more need to fight over, run from, or justify and defend what you think you don't deserve. How have you defended or ran from what you think you don't deserve? What did it look like? What can you do differently?

_____
_____
_____
_____
_____
_____
_____
_____
_____
_____
_____
_____
_____
_____
_____
_____
_____
_____
_____
_____
_____
_____

Notes:

Business Ideas

Goals

Action Steps

Successes

Your self-doubt, unworthiness, false humility, fear of what others think of you and more is the ego—your false self. It's not you. What will happen in your business as you realize that self-doubt and unworthiness aren't yours to own?

_____
_____
_____
_____
_____
_____
_____
_____
_____
_____
_____
_____
_____
_____
_____
_____
_____
_____
_____
_____
_____
_____
_____

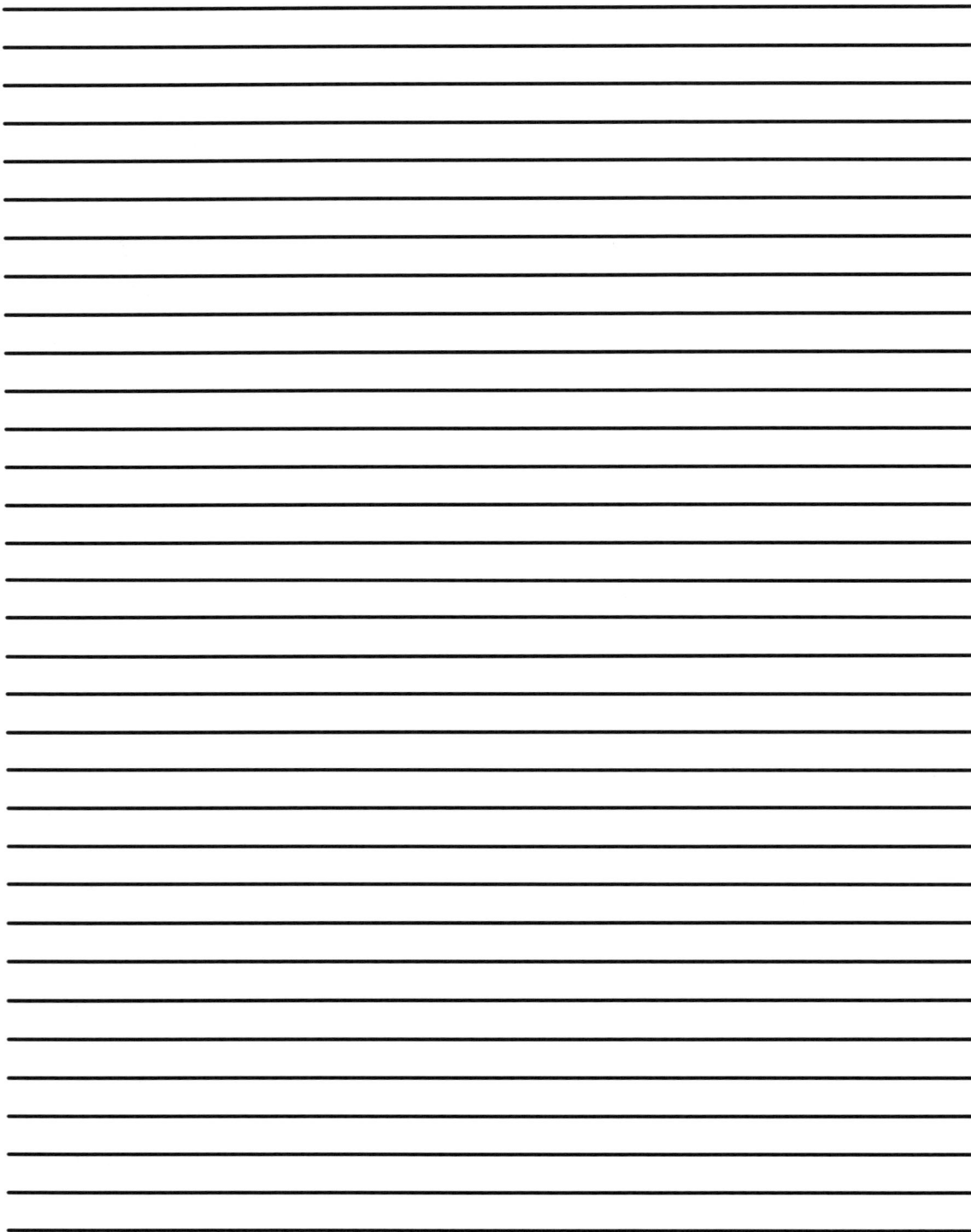

Notes:

Business Ideas

Goals

Action Steps

Successes

You are completely worthy and lovable as you are, and you owe it to yourself to keep taking steps, whether small or big steps. What would your business look like in 5 years if you take daily steps to build it? What would you do if you knew you could not fail?

_____

_____

_____

_____

_____

_____

_____

_____

_____

_____

_____

_____

_____

_____

_____

_____

_____

_____

_____

_____

_____

_____

_____

Notes:

Business Ideas

Goals

Action Steps

Successes

Save one day each week to work "on" your business when you see no clients. Reflect on what's working or not. What can you improve or automate? How can you save time? How can you make your business operate more effectively?

_____

_____

_____

_____

_____

_____

_____

_____

_____

_____

_____

_____

_____

_____

_____

_____

_____

_____

_____

_____

Notes:

Business Ideas

Goals

Action Steps

Successes

NBOs who can't receive money can't be examples for others to follow. How will you feel when receiving money is no longer an issue?

_____
_____
_____
_____
_____
_____
_____
_____
_____
_____
_____
_____
_____
_____
_____
_____
_____
_____
_____
_____
_____
_____
_____
_____

Notes:

Business Ideas

Goals

Action Steps

Successes

Systems keep you on track, save you time, protect your self-worth, command respect from others, and generate predictable and consistent sales. Are there repetitive tasks in your business? How could you automate things to go more smoothly?

_____
_____
_____
_____
_____
_____
_____
_____
_____
_____
_____
_____
_____
_____
_____
_____
_____
_____
_____
_____
_____
_____
_____
_____

Notes:

Business Ideas

Goals

Action Steps

Successes

Qualify your business decisions. Even a wise purchase at the
wrong timing can kill your business. Is this purchase a need or a
want? Do I need it now, or in the future?
Ask respected opinions.

_____

_____

_____

_____

_____

_____

_____

_____

_____

_____

_____

_____

_____

_____

_____

_____

_____

_____

_____

_____

_____

_____

_____

Notes:

Business Ideas

Goals

Action Steps

Successes

If you say you want business growth, more success, more money, but you're not allowing it, you need to ask yourself: What am I getting out of staying where I am? Safety? Convenience? Why are your actions not matching what you say you want?

_____

_____

_____

_____

_____

_____

_____

_____

_____

_____

_____

_____

_____

_____

_____

_____

_____

_____

_____

_____

Notes:

Business Ideas

Goals

Action Steps

Successes

Value add-on bonuses give clients extra value without committing more of your time. If you feel tempted to lower your prices, or if the client asks for a discount, offer a value add-on bonus instead. What value add-on bonuses can you create for clients?

_____
_____
_____
_____
_____
_____
_____
_____
_____
_____
_____
_____
_____
_____
_____
_____
_____
_____
_____
_____
_____
_____
_____

Notes:

Business Ideas

Goals

Action Steps

Successes

Always print your prices on paper; you'll be less likely to negotiate your self-worth in front of the client. What other systems can you create to protect your self-worth?

_____

_____

_____

_____

_____

_____

_____

_____

_____

_____

_____

_____

_____

_____

_____

_____

_____

_____

_____

_____

_____

_____

Notes:

Business Ideas

Goals

Action Steps

Successes

Money loves structure. The better you illustrate your services online and in person, the more clients will trust and buy. There are countless ways you can create a better web presence. What will you do next?

_____

_____

_____

_____

_____

_____

_____

_____

_____

_____

_____

_____

_____

_____

_____

_____

_____

_____

_____

_____

Notes:

Business Ideas

Goals

Action Steps

Successes

Every client is a gift that yields more clarity on the type of clients you want and don't want. From your client experiences, what do you notice you would like more of? What would you like less of?

_____

_____

_____

_____

_____

_____

_____

_____

_____

_____

_____

_____

_____

_____

_____

_____

_____

_____

_____

_____

_____

_____

Notes:

Business Ideas

Goals

Action Steps

Successes

Don't try to help clients with everything. Help with issues you're best at and enjoy. What's important to you in how you work with people?

_____

_____

_____

_____

_____

_____

_____

_____

_____

_____

_____

_____

_____

_____

_____

_____

_____

_____

_____

_____

_____

_____

_____

_____

Notes:

Business Ideas

Goals

Action Steps

Successes

Ask yourself what example you want to set for your family, friends, children, grandchildren about their worth. After you pass on, what will they say about you? How will your family feel about themselves from your example? How do you want to be remembered?

_____
_____
_____
_____
_____
_____
_____
_____
_____
_____
_____
_____
_____
_____
_____
_____
_____
_____
_____
_____
_____
_____
_____
_____

Notes:

Business Ideas

Goals

Action Steps

Successes

A client who cannot prioritize working with you is not fully committed. Embrace clients who are ready to work, and let go of clients who are not ready to work. How can you better identify ideal clients and dud clients?

_____
_____
_____
_____
_____
_____
_____
_____
_____
_____
_____
_____
_____
_____
_____
_____
_____
_____
_____
_____
_____
_____

Notes:

Business Ideas

Goals

Action Steps

Successes

There's no such thing as not having enough time; it's about how people prioritize time. As your priorities change, how you spend your time changes. What priorities do you need to have scheduled?

_____

_____

_____

_____

_____

_____

_____

_____

_____

_____

_____

_____

_____

_____

_____

_____

_____

_____

_____

_____

_____

_____

Notes:

Business Ideas

Goals

Action Steps

Successes

The fear of losing approval from others is the biggest reason we self-sabotage, don't attract clients and don't sell. How will you feel when fear of losing approval is no longer an issue? What would happen in your business?

_____

_____

_____

_____

_____

_____

_____

_____

_____

_____

_____

_____

_____

_____

_____

_____

_____

_____

_____

_____

_____

_____

_____

Notes:

Business Ideas

Goals

Action Steps

Successes

Whatever level of success we allow for ourselves is a direct
reflection of our beliefs about what we feel we deserve.
How does unworthiness stop your success?
How will you know when you're breaking free from it?
How will your business be different?

_____

_____

_____

_____

_____

_____

_____

_____

_____

_____

_____

_____

_____

_____

_____

_____

_____

_____

_____

_____

Notes:

Business Ideas

Goals

Action Steps

Successes

Two of your top ten money-producing activities create 80% of
your money—prioritize those top two and deprioritize low-
return busywork. Which tasks are most important to your
business income? Which seem important, but aren't?

_____

_____

_____

_____

_____

_____

_____

_____

_____

_____

_____

_____

_____

_____

_____

_____

_____

_____

_____

_____

_____

_____

Notes:

Business Ideas

Goals

Action Steps

Successes

Anytime you're feeling fear, frustration, anger or any negativity, remember these are gifts. Ask yourself: What am I afraid of right now? What am I resisting right now? What lie am I believing about myself right now?

_____
_____
_____
_____
_____
_____
_____
_____
_____
_____
_____
_____
_____
_____
_____
_____
_____
_____
_____
_____
_____
_____

Notes:

Business Ideas

Goals

Action Steps

Successes

The ideal client must be emotionally accessible as well as accountable and taking responsibility for their change. What will ultimately happen with clients who do not fit this criteria?

_____

_____

_____

_____

_____

_____

_____

_____

_____

_____

_____

_____

_____

_____

_____

_____

_____

_____

_____

_____

_____

_____

_____

Notes:

Business Ideas

Goals

Action Steps

Successes

Schedule your sales opportunities during times of day when you have the most energy. What happens when you imagine yourself with repeated sales success? What conditions will help this to occur?

_____
_____
_____
_____
_____
_____
_____
_____
_____
_____
_____
_____
_____
_____
_____
_____
_____
_____
_____
_____
_____
_____
_____
_____

Notes:

Business Ideas

Goals

Action Steps

Successes

At the beginning of an Intake Assessment, a client who has many questions will have very few at the end of a well-conducted intake, even if you didn't answer their questions directly. Why do the client's questions reduce by the end of a well-conducted Intake?

_____
_____
_____
_____
_____
_____
_____
_____
_____
_____
_____
_____
_____
_____
_____
_____
_____
_____
_____
_____
_____
_____
_____

Notes:

Business Ideas

Goals

Action Steps

Successes

Stay in the driver's seat. If the client asks the majority of the questions, you've lost control and the client is not emotionally engaged. What will happen if the client isn't emotionally engaged during your Intake?

_____
_____
_____
_____
_____
_____
_____
_____
_____
_____
_____
_____
_____
_____
_____
_____
_____
_____
_____
_____
_____
_____
_____

Notes:

Business Ideas

Goals

Action Steps

Successes

Always use the same Intake questions for each client and write in client answers on your intake sheet. Why is it important to use the same questions with all clients? What will happen if you don't do this?

_____

_____

_____

_____

_____

_____

_____

_____

_____

_____

_____

_____

_____

_____

_____

_____

_____

_____

_____

_____

_____

_____

_____

Notes:

Business Ideas

Goals

Action Steps

Successes

Unless your gut is telling you not to work with a client, always ask for the sale. What thoughts might stop you from asking from the sale?

_____

_____

_____

_____

_____

_____

_____

_____

_____

_____

_____

_____

_____

_____

_____

_____

_____

_____

_____

_____

_____

_____

Notes:

Business Ideas

Goals

Action Steps

Successes

Focus on three things when selling: asking key questions,
engaging the client emotionally, and listening compassionately.
What would happen if you didn't?

_____

_____

_____

_____

_____

_____

_____

_____

_____

_____

_____

_____

_____

_____

_____

_____

_____

_____

_____

_____

_____

_____

Notes:

Business Ideas

Goals

Action Steps

Successes

Clients who want quick fixes either aren't ready or haven't been qualified to do long-term transformative work. How might you identify a quick-fix client vs. a long-term client?

_____

_____

_____

_____

_____

_____

_____

_____

_____

_____

_____

_____

_____

_____

_____

_____

_____

_____

_____

_____

_____

Notes:

Business Ideas

Goals

Action Steps

Successes

Most of your non-sales will be because the client bought into their expectations before you helped them reach their emotional reasons for seeking your services. Why should you encourage clients to work with you only after you've helped them reach their emotional reasons, and not based on their expectations of the service?

_____
_____
_____
_____
_____
_____
_____
_____
_____
_____
_____
_____
_____
_____
_____
_____
_____
_____
_____
_____
_____

Notes:

Business Ideas

Goals

Action Steps

Successes

If the client shows you they are responsible, accountable and puts into practice your guidance, they earn the privilege to work with you for the longer term. What kinds of service packages might you design for highly accountable clients? Less accountable clients?

_____
_____
_____
_____
_____
_____
_____
_____
_____
_____
_____
_____
_____
_____
_____
_____
_____
_____
_____
_____
_____
_____

Notes:

Business Ideas

Goals

Action Steps

Successes

It's your job to determine the client's priority level and commitment level in your first conversation as best as you can. What types of things might a potentially committed client say during their intake? What about an uncommitted client?

_____

_____

_____

_____

_____

_____

_____

_____

_____

_____

_____

_____

_____

_____

_____

_____

_____

_____

_____

_____

_____

_____

_____

Notes:

Business Ideas

Goals

Action Steps

Successes

Giving consistent homework to your clients provides better service value and creates client accountability. What homework can you give to clients? (i.e. assessments, inventories, workbook exercises, quizzes, handouts, videos and audios.)

_____
_____
_____
_____
_____
_____
_____
_____
_____
_____
_____
_____
_____
_____
_____
_____
_____
_____
_____
_____
_____
_____
_____
_____

Notes:

Business Ideas

Goals

Action Steps

Successes

The client is showing interest in your service package, but hesitates when offered the sale. Why does asking the client "If money were no object, which of these packages would you want?" save you so much time and energy?

_____

_____

_____

_____

_____

_____

_____

_____

_____

_____

_____

_____

_____

_____

_____

_____

_____

_____

_____

_____

_____

_____

Notes:

Business Ideas

Goals

Action Steps

Successes

Don't mix coaching with an Intake Assessment. Never give the client the impression that you're going to do therapy or coaching during your Intake. What will most likely happen in your business if you mix coaching/healing work with your client's Intake Assessment?

_____
_____
_____
_____
_____
_____
_____
_____
_____
_____
_____
_____
_____
_____
_____
_____
_____
_____
_____
_____
_____

Notes:

Business Ideas

Goals

Action Steps

Successes

Always ask your key questions before you explain the details of your business. What will happen if you explain the details of your business before you ask your key questions?

_____
_____
_____
_____
_____
_____
_____
_____
_____
_____
_____
_____
_____
_____
_____
_____
_____
_____
_____
_____
_____
_____
_____

Notes:

Business Ideas

Goals

Action Steps

Successes

If the client isn't applying what you're working on in between package sessions, you likely didn't qualify the client properly, or didn't express what the package is for and outline how it is to be used. What makes utilizing a package of sessions correctly so beneficial for client transformation?

_____
_____
_____
_____
_____
_____
_____
_____
_____
_____
_____
_____
_____
_____
_____
_____
_____
_____
_____
_____
_____
_____

Notes:

Business Ideas

Goals

Action Steps

Successes

Discounting prices for clients who are in fear (not hopeful) when you offer the sale pulls you into their victimhood. Instead of discounting, offer value add-on incentives. What's the difference between being charitable and enabling victimhood?

_____
_____
_____
_____
_____
_____
_____
_____
_____
_____
_____
_____
_____
_____
_____
_____
_____
_____
_____
_____
_____
_____
_____
_____
_____
_____

Notes:

Business Ideas

Goals

Action Steps

Successes

Study how many sessions clients have needed to get desired results and continually sharpen your packages. What long-term transformation could you offer to your clients that you're not currently offering?

_____

_____

_____

_____

_____

_____

_____

_____

_____

_____

_____

_____

_____

_____

_____

_____

_____

_____

_____

_____

_____

Notes:

Business Ideas

Goals

Action Steps

Successes

When you offer your sale and your client says, "Can I think about it?" it means you didn't properly qualify them or they have unaddressed concerns. How will you know when your Intake questions are emotionally engaging the client?

_____
_____
_____
_____
_____
_____
_____
_____
_____
_____
_____
_____
_____
_____
_____
_____
_____
_____
_____
_____
_____
_____
_____

Notes:

Business Ideas

Goals

Action Steps

Successes

Posture the client correctly via your systems and online
presence before they come into your office for the first time.
What is likely to occur if the client doesn't consume content
you've provided online about you and your business
before their first visit?

_____
_____
_____
_____
_____
_____
_____
_____
_____
_____
_____
_____
_____
_____
_____
_____
_____
_____
_____
_____
_____

Notes:

Business Ideas

Goals

Action Steps

Successes

Your questions invite the clients to look deeper within themselves and feel the truth about their current state so they can emotionally reconnect with why they made the appointment. What would happen if clients didn't emotionally reconnect with their "why"?

_____
_____
_____
_____
_____
_____
_____
_____
_____
_____
_____
_____
_____
_____
_____
_____
_____
_____
_____
_____
_____
_____

Notes:

Business Ideas

Goals

Action Steps

Successes

You are the authority in your business. You set the terms for how you want to work with clients. What are you like when you're at your best? How can you craft your session packages accordingly?

_____
_____
_____
_____
_____
_____
_____
_____
_____
_____
_____
_____
_____
_____
_____
_____
_____
_____
_____
_____
_____
_____
_____

Notes:

Business Ideas

Goals

Action Steps

Successes

What ultimately determines session prices: market average for your service, clients' willingness to pay, extra value given beyond clients' expectations, and providing outstanding results. What will you do when you have enough money?

_____

_____

_____

_____

_____

_____

_____

_____

_____

_____

_____

_____

_____

_____

_____

_____

_____

_____

_____

_____

_____

_____

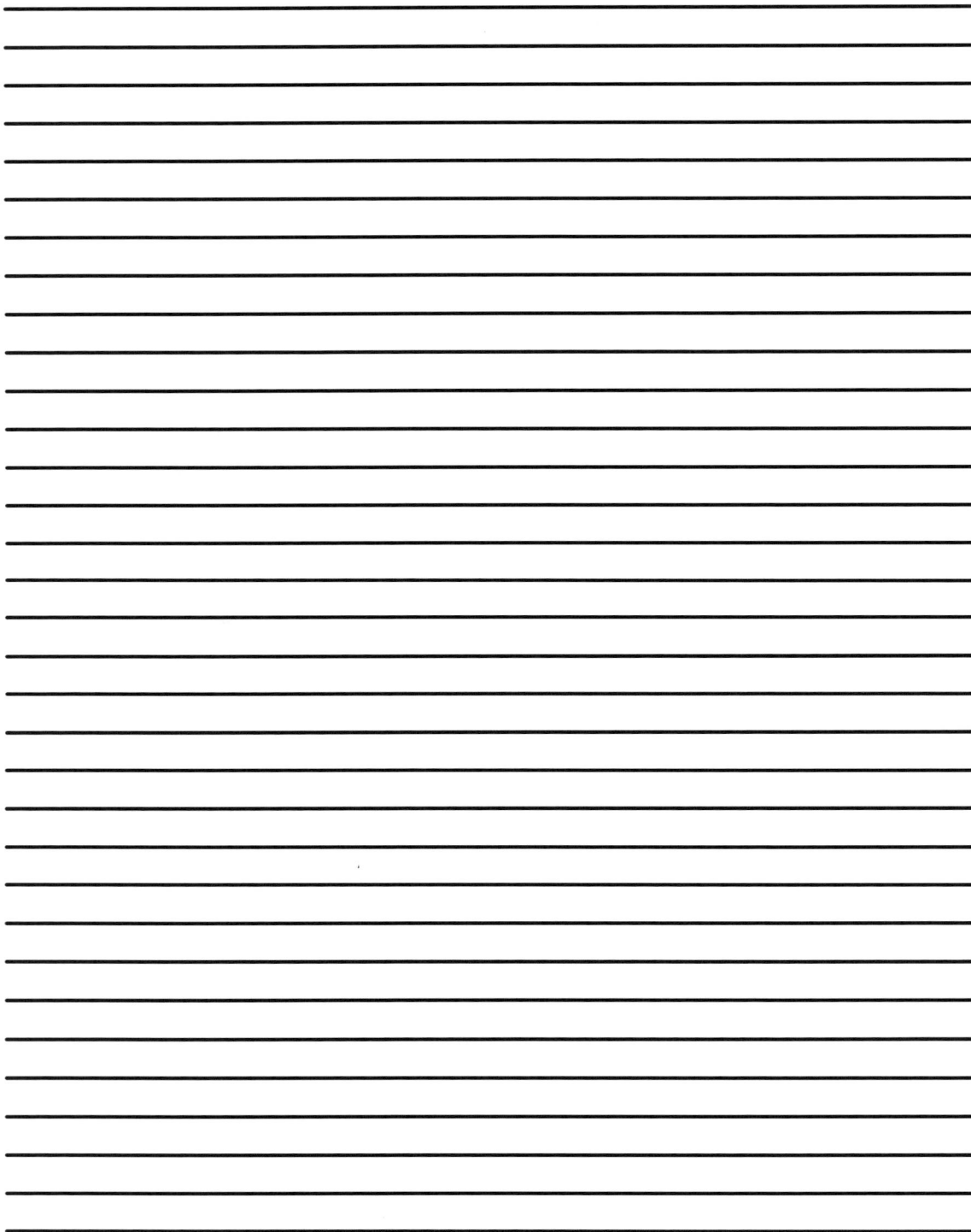

Notes:

Business Ideas

Goals

Action Steps

Successes

Your price points qualify ideal clients, disqualify dud clients, and preserve your self-worth. How do your price points do all of this? Why should you look at pricing as a client qualifier?

_____
_____
_____
_____
_____
_____
_____
_____
_____
_____
_____
_____
_____
_____
_____
_____
_____
_____
_____
_____
_____
_____
_____
_____

Notes:

Business Ideas

Goals

Action Steps

Successes

Your business will not outgrow your ability to sell. How will you know when your ability to sell is no longer a concern?

_____

_____

_____

_____

_____

_____

_____

_____

_____

_____

_____

_____

_____

_____

_____

_____

_____

_____

_____

_____

_____

_____

_____

_____

Notes:

Business Ideas

Goals

Action Steps

Successes

At the Intake Assessment you ask your key questions, and it's the most important system in your business. How will you know when you are consistently conducting your Intake assessment correctly?

_____

_____

_____

_____

_____

_____

_____

_____

_____

_____

_____

_____

_____

_____

_____

_____

_____

_____

_____

_____

_____

_____

Notes:

Business Ideas

Goals

Action Steps

Successes

The Intake invites the client to get out of lying behaviors (fear, denial) so that you can discover if they can tell you their truth. What will happen if you sell to a client who cannot speak their truth?

_____

_____

_____

_____

_____

_____

_____

_____

_____

_____

_____

_____

_____

_____

_____

_____

_____

_____

_____

_____

_____

_____

_____

_____

Notes:

Business Ideas

Goals

Action Steps

Successes

After you ask a closing question, be quiet and wait for the client to answer. Why should you wait? What does the compulsion to keep explaining when you should be quiet come from?

_____

_____

_____

_____

_____

_____

_____

_____

_____

_____

_____

_____

_____

_____

_____

_____

_____

_____

_____

_____

_____

_____

Notes:

Business Ideas

Goals

Action Steps

Successes

Even if you don't have another client afterward, always stop your sessions on time. The clock is your friend, not your enemy. Why is it so important to self-worth and professionalism to stay on time with clients?

_____

_____

_____

_____

_____

_____

_____

_____

_____

_____

_____

_____

_____

_____

_____

_____

_____

_____

_____

_____

_____

_____

_____

Notes:

Business Ideas

Goals

Action Steps

Successes

Before signing a formal office lease, make sure you have a regular stream of paying clientele and make sure you know how to sell. How are you ensuring that your income/expenses are justifying your expansion?

_____

_____

_____

_____

_____

_____

_____

_____

_____

_____

_____

_____

_____

_____

_____

_____

_____

_____

_____

_____

_____

_____

Notes:

Business Ideas

Goals

Action Steps

Successes

Set up your 'Google My Business' account and ask clients for honest reviews consistently. More Google reviews means better business visibility. Request one Google review from a client weekly.

_____
_____
_____
_____
_____
_____
_____
_____
_____
_____
_____
_____
_____
_____
_____
_____
_____
_____
_____
_____
_____
_____
_____
_____
_____

Notes:

Business Ideas

Goals

Action Steps

Successes

Made in the USA
Las Vegas, NV
20 August 2022